JAVA ESSENTIALS : LEARN THE BASICS IN A WEEKEND

Deepesh Rastogi

Table of Contents

1. **Introduction to Java**
   - What is Java?
   - History and Evolution
   - Features of Java
2. **Getting Started**
   - Setting Up Your Java Environment
   - Installing the Java Development Kit (JDK)
   - Setting Up an Integrated Development Environment (IDE)
   - Writing Your First Java Program
3. **Basic Syntax and Structure**
   - Understanding Java Syntax
   - Data Types and Variables
   - Operators in Java
   - Control Flow Statements
4. **Working with Data**
   - Arrays and Strings
   - Collections Framework Overview
   - Using Lists, Sets, and Maps
5. **Object-Oriented Programming Concepts**
   - Classes and Objects
   - Inheritance and Polymorphism
   - Encapsulation and Abstraction
   - Interfaces and Abstract Classes
6. **Exception Handling**
   - Understanding Exceptions
   - Try-Catch Blocks
   - Creating Custom Exceptions
7. **Basic Input and Output**

- Reading from and Writing to the Console
- File I/O Basics
- Using Java's I/O Libraries

8. **Java Development Best Practices**
   - Code Conventions and Formatting
   - Debugging Techniques
   - Writing Clean and Maintainable Code

9. **Next Steps in Java Development**
   - Learning Resources and Communities
   - Advanced Java Concepts to Explore
   - Building Your Portfolio and Projects

10. **Conclusion**
    - Recap of Key Concepts
    - Staying Motivated and Continuing Your Learning Journey

Introduction of Book

Welcome to *Java Essentials: Learn the Basics in a Weekend*! This book is designed for beginners eager to dive into the world of Java programming. In just two days, you'll grasp the fundamental concepts of Java, from basic syntax to object-oriented programming. With clear explanations, practical examples, and hands-on exercises, you'll build a strong foundation that prepares you for further exploration in the Java ecosystem. Whether you're looking to enhance your career or embark on a new hobby, this guide will equip you with the essential skills to start your Java journey with confidence. Let's get started!

Acknowledgments

Thank you for joining me on this journey through *Java Essentials: Learn the Basics in a Weekend*! I appreciate your commitment to enhancing your programming skills. Special thanks to the countless developers and educators who inspired this book with their passion and insights. Your contributions to the programming community have paved the way for learners everywhere. I also want to acknowledge friends and family for their unwavering support during the writing process. Remember, the journey doesn't end here—continue exploring, experimenting, and growing in your Java skills. I wish you all the best in your programming endeavors!

Chapter 1: Introduction to Java

What is Java?

Java is a high-level, object-oriented programming language developed by Sun Microsystems in the mid-1990s. It was designed with the principle of "write once, run anywhere," which means that Java code can be executed on any device that has a Java Virtual Machine (JVM), regardless of the underlying hardware and operating system. This portability has made Java one of the most popular programming languages in the world.

Java's syntax is similar to C and C++, making it easier for developers familiar with those languages to transition to Java. It emphasizes simplicity, security, and reliability, which is essential for developing robust applications. Java is widely used for building web applications, mobile applications (especially on Android), server-side applications, and large-scale enterprise systems.

Java's ecosystem includes a vast array of libraries, frameworks, and tools that enhance its capabilities and facilitate development. Some of the notable frameworks include Spring for web applications, Hibernate for data access, and JavaFX for rich client applications.

History and Evolution

Java was initially developed by James Gosling and his team at Sun Microsystems in 1991. Originally called "Oak," the language was intended for interactive television but was deemed too advanced for the digital cable television industry of the time. In 1995, Oak was renamed Java, inspired by Java coffee, and it was released as a core component of the Java Platform.

Java's first major version, Java 1.0, was introduced in 1996, and it quickly gained popularity due to its promise of platform independence and its appeal to internet developers. The rise of the internet in the late 1990s propelled Java into the spotlight, particularly with the introduction of applets—small Java programs that could run in web browsers.

As Java evolved, it saw the release of several major versions:

- **Java 2 (1998)**: Introduced the Java 2 Platform, which included the Java Foundation Classes (JFC), the Swing graphical user interface (GUI) toolkit, and the Collections Framework.
- **Java 5 (2004)**: Also known as Java 1.5, it introduced major language enhancements such as generics, annotations, enumerated types, and the enhanced for loop, making Java more powerful and easier to use.

- **Java 8 (2014)**: This version introduced lambda expressions, the Stream API, and the java.time package for date and time manipulation, significantly enhancing Java's capabilities for functional programming.
- **Java 9 (2017)**: Introduced the module system (Project Jigsaw), which allows developers to modularize their applications for better maintainability.
- **Java 11 (2018)**: A Long-Term Support (LTS) release, it included several new features, such as the HTTP Client API and various performance improvements.
- **Java 17 (2021)**: Another LTS release, it brought in pattern matching for `instanceof`, sealed classes, and significant enhancements in garbage collection and performance.

Over the years, Java has become a mature language, supported by a robust community and numerous resources for learning and development. Its evolution has focused on maintaining backward compatibility while incorporating new features and improvements that align with modern programming practices.

Features of Java

Java is known for its rich set of features that make it a versatile language for various types of applications. Here are some of its key features:

1. Object-Oriented Programming (OOP)

Java is fundamentally object-oriented, which means it allows developers to create modular programs using objects that encapsulate data and behavior. OOP principles such as inheritance, encapsulation, polymorphism, and abstraction enable code reuse and make software development more manageable.

2. Platform Independence

One of Java's most significant advantages is its platform independence. Java code is compiled into bytecode, which can run on any machine equipped with a JVM. This feature is crucial for developers who want their applications to be usable across different platforms without modification.

3. Automatic Memory Management

Java provides automatic garbage collection, which means that the JVM automatically manages memory allocation and deallocation. This reduces the risk of memory leaks and other memory-related issues that can arise in languages requiring manual memory management.

4. Rich Standard Library

Java comes with a comprehensive standard library that provides a wide range of built-in classes and methods for handling tasks such as data manipulation, networking, file I/O, and graphical user interface (GUI) development. This library significantly accelerates the development process by providing reusable components.

5. Security Features

Java was designed with security in mind. The language provides several features to create secure applications, such as the Java security manager, bytecode verification, and a robust access control mechanism. These features help prevent unauthorized access and ensure that applications run safely.

6. Multithreading Support

Java supports multithreading, which allows developers to create applications that can perform multiple tasks simultaneously. This feature is particularly useful for developing high-performance applications, such as games and real-time data processing systems.

7. High Performance

While Java is an interpreted language, its performance has improved significantly over the years due to just-in-time (JIT) compilation and advanced optimization techniques used in the JVM. This means that Java applications can run efficiently and compete with those written in lower-level languages.

8. Robustness and Reliability

Java emphasizes strong error checking and exception handling. The language's strict syntax rules and runtime checks make it less prone to crashes and bugs. Developers can handle errors gracefully, improving the reliability of Java applications.

9. Community and Ecosystem

Java boasts a vast community of developers and a rich ecosystem of frameworks, libraries, and tools. This support network is invaluable for newcomers and experienced developers alike, providing a wealth of resources for learning, problem-solving, and collaboration.

Summary

Java's journey from its inception in the early 1990s to its status as one of the most widely used programming languages today is a testament to its robustness, versatility, and adaptability. By understanding what Java is, its history, its core features, and how to set up your development environment, you're well on your way to becoming proficient in Java programming. As you continue through this book, you'll delve deeper into the language and explore its vast capabilities, empowering you to create your own applications and solve complex problems.

Chapter 2: Getting Started

Setting Up Your Java Environment

To start programming in Java, you need to set up your development environment. This process typically involves installing the Java Development Kit (JDK) and choosing an Integrated Development Environment (IDE) to write and run your code.

1. Installing the Java Development Kit (JDK)

The JDK is essential for Java development. It includes the Java Runtime Environment (JRE), the compiler, and various tools necessary for developing Java applications.

Steps to Install the JDK:

- **Download the JDK**: Visit the official Oracle website or the OpenJDK website to download the latest version of the JDK suitable for your operating system (Windows, macOS, or Linux).

- **Run the Installer**: Follow the installation instructions. For Windows, this usually involves double-clicking the downloaded file and following the prompts. On macOS, you might need to drag the JDK to your Applications folder.
- **Set Environment Variables** (Windows): After installation, you may need to set the `JAVA_HOME` environment variable to point to your JDK installation directory. This allows other tools and IDEs to locate the JDK.
- **Verify Installation**: Open a command prompt or terminal and type `java -version` and `javac -version`. If both commands return version numbers, your JDK is installed correctly.

2. Choosing an Integrated Development Environment (IDE)

An IDE provides a user-friendly environment for writing, debugging, and managing Java code. Several IDEs are available, each with unique features. Here are some popular options:

- **Eclipse**: A powerful, open-source IDE that supports various programming languages, including Java. It offers a rich set of plugins and tools for web development, mobile development, and more.
- **IntelliJ IDEA**: A widely used IDE known for its smart code completion, powerful

refactoring tools, and user-friendly interface. The Community Edition is free and sufficient for most Java development tasks.
- **NetBeans**: Another open-source IDE that provides comprehensive tools for Java development. It's easy to use and integrates well with various Java technologies.

Setting Up Your IDE:

- **Download and Install the IDE**: Visit the official website of your chosen IDE and download the installer. Follow the installation prompts.
- **Configure the IDE**: Open your IDE and configure it to use the installed JDK. Most IDEs will automatically detect the JDK installation, but you might need to specify the path manually in the IDE settings.
- **Create a New Project**: Most IDEs allow you to create new projects through a simple wizard. Follow the prompts to set up your first Java project.

3. Writing Your First Java Program

Now that your environment is set up, you can write your first Java program. Open your IDE, create a new Java class, and enter the following code:

```
public class HelloWorld {
    public static void main(String[] args) {
```

```
        System.out.println("Hello,
World!");
    }
}
```

Save the file as `HelloWorld.java`, then compile and run it using the IDE's built-in tools. If everything is set up correctly, you should see the output:

Hello, World!

Full Program Structure

Putting it all together, this program defines a class named `HelloWorld` and contains a `main` method that outputs "Hello, World!" to the console when executed. Here's a simple step-by-step of what happens when you run this program:

1. The Java Virtual Machine (JVM) looks for the `main` method to start executing the program.
2. The `main` method is invoked.
3. The line `System.out.println("Hello, World!");` executes, sending the string "Hello, World!" to the console.
4. The program finishes execution.

Chapter 3: Basic Syntax and Structure

Java is a versatile programming language known for its robustness and simplicity. Understanding its basic syntax and structure is essential for beginners and experienced programmers alike. In this chapter, we will explore four core topics: Java syntax, data types and variables, operators, and control flow statements. Each section will provide you with the foundational knowledge necessary to write effective Java programs.

Understanding Java Syntax

What is Syntax?

In programming, syntax refers to the set of rules that defines the combinations of symbols and words that are considered valid statements in a language. Just as grammar is essential for constructing sentences in human languages, syntax is crucial for writing instructions that a computer can understand.

Java Syntax Basics

1. **Case Sensitivity**: Java is case-sensitive, which means that uppercase and lowercase letters are treated differently. For instance,

`Variable` and `variable` would be considered two distinct identifiers.

2. **Statements**: A statement is a complete instruction in Java that performs an action. Each statement ends with a semicolon (;).

    For example:

    System.out.println("Hello, World!");

3. **Whitespace**: Whitespace (spaces, tabs, and newlines) is ignored by the Java compiler, which means it can be used to enhance the readability of the code. For instance:

    int x = 5; // This is valid
    int y = 10; // This is also valid

4. **Comments**: Comments are used to annotate code and are ignored during execution. Java supports single-line comments (//) and multi-line comments (/* */).

    // This is a single-line comment

    /* This is a multi-line comment */

5. **Identifiers**: Identifiers are names given to variables, classes, methods, and other entities in Java. They must start with a letter, dollar sign ($), or underscore (_) and can contain letters,

digits, dollar signs, and underscores. However, they cannot begin with a digit. For example:

int myVariable; // Valid identifier

int 1stVariable; // Invalid identifier

6. **Keywords**: Java has a set of reserved words known as keywords that have special meanings and cannot be used as identifiers. Examples include `int`, `class`, `public`, and `void`.

Java Program Structure

A basic Java program consists of the following components:

- **Class Declaration**: Every Java application must have at least one class. A class serves as a blueprint for creating objects.
- **Main Method**: The `main` method is the entry point of the program, where the execution begins.
- **Statements**: Inside the `main` method (or any method), you can include statements that perform actions.

Here's a simple example of a complete Java program structure:

```
public class MyFirstProgram {
        public static void main(String[] args) {
        System.out.println("Welcome to Java!");
        }
}
```

In this example:

- `public class MyFirstProgram` declares a class named `MyFirstProgram`.
- `public static void main(String[] args)` declares the main method.
- `System.out.println("Welcome to Java!");` is a statement that prints text to the console.

Understanding this structure is fundamental for writing any Java program.

Class Declaration

- **`public`**: This is an access modifier that means this class can be accessed from any other class. It's a way to control visibility in Java.
- **`class`**: This keyword is used to declare a class, which is a fundamental concept in object-oriented programming. A class is a blueprint for creating objects (instances).
- **`HelloWorld`**: This is the name of the class. By convention, class names in Java start with an uppercase letter. The name should reflect the

purpose of the class, and in this case, it indicates that this class will output "Hello, World!".

Main Method Declaration

- `public`: Again, this access modifier indicates that the method can be called from anywhere.
- `static`: This keyword means that the method belongs to the class itself rather than an instance of the class. You can call this method without creating an object of the class.
- `void`: This indicates that the method does not return any value.
- `main`: This is the name of the method. In Java, the `main` method is the entry point of any standalone application; it's where the program begins execution.
- `String[] args`: This is an array of `String` objects. It allows the program to accept command-line arguments. When you run the program, you can pass strings to it via the command line, and those strings will be available in this array

Printing to the Console

- **`System.out`**: This is a standard output stream in Java. `System` is a built-in class that provides access to system-level operations, and `out` is a static member of the `System` class that represents the standard output (usually the console).
- **`println`**: This is a method of the `PrintStream` class, which is the type of `out`. The `println` method prints the given message to the console and then moves the cursor to a new line.

`"Hello, World!"`: This is the string that will be printed. It's enclosed in double quotes, indicating that it's a string literal.

Data Types and Variables

What are Data Types?

Data types in Java define the type of data that a variable can hold. They determine the operations that can be performed on the data and the amount of memory allocated for it. Java is a statically typed language, meaning that data types must be declared explicitly.

Primitive Data Types

Java has eight primitive data types:

1. **byte**: An 8-bit signed integer. Range: -128 to 127.

    byte b = 100;

2. **short**: A 16-bit signed integer. Range: -32,768 to 32,767.

    short s = 10000;

3. **int**: A 32-bit signed integer. Range: -2^{31} to $2^{31}-1$.

    int i = 123456789;

4. **long**: A 64-bit signed integer. Range: -2^{63} to $2^{63}-1$.

    long l = 12345678901L;
    // 'L' suffix indicates long

5. **float**: A single-precision 32-bit IEEE 754 floating point. Used for decimal values.

    float f = 10.5f;
    // 'f' suffix indicates float

6. **double**: A double-precision 64-bit IEEE 754 floating point. It is the default type for decimal values.

```
double d = 20.99;
```

7. **char**: A single 16-bit Unicode character.

   ```
   char c = 'A';
   ```

8. **boolean**: Represents one of two values: `true` or `false`.

   ```
   boolean isJavaFun = true;
   ```

Reference Data Types

In addition to primitive types, Java also supports reference data types, which refer to objects. Reference types include:

- **Classes**: Objects created from class definitions.
- **Interfaces**: Abstract types that define method signatures but not implementations.
- **Arrays**: A collection of elements of the same type.

For example, creating a string (a reference type):

```
String greeting = "Hello, World!";
```

Variables

A variable is a container for storing data values. To declare a variable in Java, specify its data type followed by the variable name:

```
int age; // Declaration
age = 25; // Initialization
```

You can also declare and initialize a variable in one line:

```
int age = 25; // Declaration and initialization
```

Variable naming conventions:

- Use meaningful names that reflect the purpose of the variable (e.g., `studentName`).
- Follow camelCase naming convention for multi-word identifiers.
- Avoid using reserved keywords as variable names.

Operators in Java

Operators are special symbols that perform operations on variables and values. Java provides a rich set of operators, which can be classified into several categories:

1. Arithmetic Operators

Arithmetic operators are used to perform mathematical operations:

- **Addition (+)**: Adds two operands.
- **Subtraction (-)**: Subtracts the second operand from the first.
- **Multiplication (*)**: Multiplies two operands.
- **Division (/)**: Divides the first operand by the second.
- **Modulus (%)**: Returns the remainder of a division operation.

Example:

```
int a = 10;
int b = 3;
int sum = a + b; // 13
int difference = a - b; // 7
int product = a * b; // 30
int quotient = a / b; // 3
int remainder = a % b; // 1
```

2. Relational Operators

Relational operators are used to compare two values and return a boolean result (`true` or `false`):

- **Equal to (==)**: Checks if two operands are equal.
- **Not equal to (!=)**: Checks if two operands are not equal.

- **Greater than (>)**: Checks if the left operand is greater than the right.
- **Less than (<)**: Checks if the left operand is less than the right.
- **Greater than or equal to (>=)**: Checks if the left operand is greater than or equal to the right.
- **Less than or equal to (<=)**: Checks if the left operand is less than or equal to the right.

Example:

int x = 5;

int y = 10;

boolean isEqual = (x == y); // false

boolean isGreater = (x > y); // false

3. Logical Operators

Logical operators are used to combine boolean expressions:

- **Logical AND (&&)**: Returns true if both operands are true.
- **Logical OR (||)**: Returns true if at least one operand is true.
- **Logical NOT (!)**: Reverses the boolean value of its operand.

Example:

boolean a = true;

boolean b = false;

boolean resultAnd = (a && b); // false

boolean resultOr = (a || b); // true

boolean resultNot = !a; // false

4. Assignment Operators

Assignment operators are used to assign values to variables:

- **Simple Assignment (=)**: Assigns the value of the right operand to the left operand.
- **Addition Assignment (+=)**: Adds the right operand to the left operand and assigns the result to the left.
- **Subtraction Assignment (-=)**: Subtracts the right operand from the left and assigns the result to the left.
- **Multiplication Assignment (*=)**: Multiplies the left operand by the right and assigns the result to the left.
- **Division Assignment (/=)**: Divides the left operand by the right and assigns the result to the left.

- **Modulus Assignment (%=)**: Applies the modulus operator and assigns the result to the left.

Example:

int number = 10;

number += 5; // number = 15

number -= 3; // number = 12

5. Unary Operators

Unary operators operate on a single operand:

- **Unary Plus (+)**: Indicates a positive value (generally not needed).
- **Unary Minus (-)**: Negates the value of the operand.
- **Increment (++)**: Increases the value of a variable by 1.
- **Decrement (--)**: Decreases the value of a variable by 1.

Example:

int num = 5;
num++; // num becomes 6
num--; // num becomes 5

6. Ternary Operator

The ternary operator (? :) is a shorthand for `if-else` statements. It takes three operands and evaluates a boolean expression. If the expression is true, it returns the first value; otherwise, it returns the second value.

Example:

```
int a = 10;
int b = 20;
int max = (a > b) ? a : b; // max becomes 20
```

Control Flow Statements

Control flow statements determine the order in which statements are executed in a program. Java provides several control flow statements, including conditional statements and loops. In this section, we will focus on conditional statements, specifically `if` and `switch`.

1. `if` Statement

The `if` statement allows you to execute a block of code based on a specified condition. If the condition evaluates to true, the block of code is executed; if false, it is skipped.

Basic syntax:

```
if (condition) { // Code to execute if condition is true }
```

Example:

```
int score = 85;
```

```
if (score >= 60) { System.out.println("You passed!"); }
```

`if-else` Statement

You can extend the `if` statement to include an `else` block, which executes when the condition is false.

Example:

```
int score = 45;
```

```
if (score >= 60) {
        System.out.println("You passed!"); } else {
        System.out.println("You failed.");
}
```

`if-else if-else` Statement

For multiple conditions, you can use `else if` to check additional conditions.

Example:

int score = 75;

if (score >= 90) { System.out.println("Grade: A"); }

2. `switch` Statement

The `switch` statement is another control flow statement that allows you to execute one block of code among many alternatives based on the value of an expression. It is typically used when you have multiple conditions based on the same variable.

Basic syntax:

```
switch (expression) {
case value1: // Code to execute if expression == value1
break;
case value2: // Code to execute if expression == value2
break;
// You can have any number of case statements default:
// Code to execute if no case matches
}
```

Example :

```
int day = 3; switch (day) {
case 1: System.out.println("Monday"); break;
case 2: System.out.println("Tuesday"); break;
case 3: System.out.println("Wednesday"); break;
default: System.out.println("Invalid day"); }
```

In this example, if `day` equals 3, the output will be "Wednesday." The `break` statement is crucial as it prevents the execution from falling through to subsequent cases.

Loops in Java

In Java, loops are control flow statements that allow code to be executed repeatedly based on a condition. The main types of loops are:

1. **For Loop**: Executes a block of code a specific number of times. It's defined with an initialization, a condition, and an increment/decrement.

    ```
    for (int i = 0; i < 5; i++) { System.out.println(i); }
    ```

The `for` loop prints `i` ; it initializes `i` at 0, checks if `i` is less than 5, and increments `i` after each iteration.

2. **While Loop**: Continues executing as long as a specified condition is true.

int i = 0;

while (i < 5) { System.out.println(i++); }

The `while` loop prints `i` starting from 0, incrementing it until it reaches 5, exiting once the condition is false.

3. **Do-While Loop**: Similar to the while loop, but it guarantees at least one execution of the code block.

int i = 0;

do {

System.out.println(i++);

} while (i < 5);

The `do-while` loop prints `i` starting from 0, incrementing it, and guarantees execution at least once, until `i` reaches 5.

Loops are essential for tasks requiring repetition, such as iterating through arrays or collections.

Summary

In this chapter, we've covered the foundational aspects of Java syntax and structure. You learned about the basic syntax rules, how to declare and use variables, different data types, operators, and control flow statements like `if` and `switch`. This knowledge sets the stage for more advanced concepts and programming techniques as you continue your journey in learning Java. Mastering these basics is crucial for writing clear, effective, and efficient Java code. As you practice, you'll become more comfortable with these elements, paving the way for more complex programming challenges.

Chapter 4: Working with Data

In Java, effective data management is crucial for building robust applications. This chapter explores three fundamental aspects of data handling: arrays and strings, an overview of the Collections Framework, and the use of lists, sets, and maps. Understanding these concepts will enable you to store, manipulate, and manage data efficiently in your Java programs.

Arrays and Strings

Arrays

An array is a collection of elements, all of the same type, stored in contiguous memory locations. Arrays are a fundamental data structure in Java, providing a way to store multiple values in a single variable.

Declaring and Initializing Arrays

In Java, you can declare an array by specifying its type followed by square brackets. You can initialize an array in several ways:

1. **Declaration without Initialization**:

```
int[] numbers; // Declaration
```

numbers = new int[5]; // Initialization

2. **Declaration with Initialization**:

int[] numbers = new int[5]; // Declaration and initialization

3. **Using an Array Literal**:

int[] numbers = {1, 2, 3, 4, 5}; // Declaration and initialization with values

The code declares an integer array named `numbers` and initializes it to hold five integers, allocating memory for the array elements.

Accessing Array Elements

You can access array elements using their index, starting from 0:

Array Length

To get the length of an array, use the `length` property:

int length = numbers.length;

// Gets the length of the array

Iterating Over Arrays

You can iterate through an array using a `for` loop or an enhanced `for` loop:

```
for (int i = 0; i < numbers.length; i++) {
System.out.println(numbers[i]); }
```

This loop, a traditional `for` loop, iterates through the `numbers` array using an index `i`, printing each element by accessing it via its index. The loop continues until `i` equals the array's length.

```
// Enhanced for loop

for (int number : numbers) {
System.out.println(number); }
```

The second loop, known as the enhanced `for` loop (or "for-each" loop), simplifies iteration by directly accessing each element in the `numbers` array without needing an index. It automatically iterates through all elements, making the code cleaner and more readable.

Strings

Strings in Java are objects that represent sequences of characters. Unlike arrays, strings are immutable, meaning their values cannot be changed once created.

Creating Strings

You can create strings in two ways:

1. **String Literal**:

    String greeting = "Hello, World!";

2. **Using the new Keyword**:

    String greeting = new String("Hello, World!");

Common String Methods

Java provides several built-in methods for string manipulation:

Length:

int length = greeting.length();
// Gets the length of the string

Concatenation:

String message = greeting + " Welcome to Java.";

Substring

String sub = greeting.substring(0, 5);
// Gets a substring (0 to 5)

Character Extraction:

char firstChar = greeting.charAt(0);
// Gets the first character

Searching:

int index = greeting.indexOf("World");
// Finds the index of "World"

Comparing:

boolean isEqual = greeting.equals("Hello, World!");
// Checks for equality

StringBuilder and StringBuffer

For performance, especially in situations where strings are modified frequently, you can use `StringBuilder` or `StringBuffer`. Both classes provide mutable sequences of characters

StringBuilder sb = new StringBuilder("Hello");

sb.append(", World!"); // Modifies the string

String result = sb.toString(); // Converts to String

Collections Framework Overview

The Java Collections Framework (JCF) provides a set of classes and interfaces for storing and manipulating groups of objects. It includes various data structures, enabling efficient data storage and retrieval.

Key Interfaces

1. **Collection**: The root interface in the collection hierarchy.
2. **List**: An ordered collection (also known as a sequence) that allows duplicates.
3. **Set**: A collection that does not allow duplicates.
4. **Map**: An object that maps keys to values, where each key is unique.

Implementations

Java provides several implementations of these interfaces, allowing you to choose the right data structure for your needs:

- **List Implementations**:
    - **ArrayList**: Resizable array implementation of the List interface. It allows fast random access but is slower for insertions and deletions.

- **LinkedList**: A doubly-linked list implementation of the List interface. It allows for efficient insertions and deletions.

- **Set Implementations**:

  - **HashSet**: A set backed by a hash table. It allows for constant-time performance for basic operations (add, remove, contains).
  - **TreeSet**: A sorted set implementation that uses a red-black tree. It allows for sorted order traversal.

- **Map Implementations**:

  - **HashMap**: A hash table-based implementation of the Map interface. It allows for fast retrieval of values based on keys.
  - **TreeMap**: A sorted map implementation that uses a red-black tree. It maintains keys in sorted order.

Using Lists, Sets, and Maps

Lists

Lists are versatile data structures that maintain the order of elements and allow duplicates. The most commonly used implementations are `ArrayList` and `LinkedList`.

Example of Using ArrayList

```java
import java.util.ArrayList;

public class ListExample {
    public static void main(String[] args) {
        ArrayList<String> fruits = new ArrayList<>();
        fruits.add("Apple");
        fruits.add("Banana");
        fruits.add("Orange");

        System.out.println("Fruits: " + fruits);
        // Accessing elements
        String firstFruit = fruits.get(0); // Apple

        // Iterating through the list
        for (String fruit : fruits) {
            System.out.println(fruit);
        }
```

```java
    // Removing an element
    fruits.remove("Banana");
    System.out.println("After removal: " + fruits);
  }
}
```

Output :

Fruits: [Apple, Banana, Orange]

Apple

Banana

Orange

After removal: [Apple, Orange]

Explanation:

1. **First Line**: Prints the entire list of fruits, displaying all elements in square brackets.
2. **Next Lines**: Iterates through the list and prints each fruit individually.
3. **After Removal**: Removes "Banana" from the list and prints the updated list, showing only "Apple" and "Orange."

Sets

Sets are collections that do not allow duplicate elements. They are useful when you want to ensure that a collection contains only unique items.

Example of Using HashSet

```java
import java.util.HashSet;

public class SetExample {
    public static void main(String[] args) {
        HashSet<String> countries = new HashSet<>();
        countries.add("USA");
        countries.add("Canada");
        countries.add("Mexico");
        countries.add("USA"); // Duplicate, will not be added
        System.out.println("Countries: " + countries);

        // Iterating through the set
        for (String country : countries) {
            System.out.println(country);
```

         }

      }

}

Output :

Countries: [Canada, USA, Mexico]

USA

Canada

Mexico

Explanation:

1. **Countries Output**: The first line prints the entire set of countries. The order may vary because `HashSet` does not maintain any specific order. However, it will include "USA," "Canada," and "Mexico," without duplicates.
2. **Iterating Output**: The loop iterates through the set and prints each country. The order of printed countries may differ each time you run the program, as `HashSet` does not guarantee a specific order. The printed values will always include "USA," "Canada," and "Mexico," but their order may vary.

Maps

Maps store key-value pairs, where each key is unique. They are excellent for associating values with unique identifiers.

Example of Using HashMap

```java
import java.util.HashMap;

public class MapExample {

    public static void main(String[] args) {

        HashMap<String, Integer> ages = new HashMap<>();

        ages.put("Alice", 30);

        ages.put("Bob", 25);

        ages.put("Charlie", 35);

        System.out.println("Ages: " + ages);

        // Accessing values

        int aliceAge = ages.get("Alice"); // 30
```

```java
        // Iterating through the map
        for (String name : ages.keySet()) {
            System.out.println(name + " is " + ages.get(name) + " years old.");
        }
    }
}
```

Output :

Ages: {Alice=30, Bob=25, Charlie=35}
Alice is 30 years old.
Bob is 25 years old.
Charlie is 35 years old.

Explanation:

1. **Ages Output**: The first line prints the entire `HashMap`, showing the names and their corresponding ages in the format `{key=value}`. The order of entries may vary because `HashMap` does not maintain a specific order.
2. **Iterating Output**: The loop iterates through the keys (names) in the `HashMap` and prints each name along with its associated age. Each entry is formatted as "name is age

years old." The order of names printed may vary each time you run the program due to the nature of `HashMap`.

Summary

In this chapter, we explored essential concepts for working with data in Java, including arrays and strings, the Collections Framework, and the practical use of lists, sets, and maps. Arrays provide a straightforward way to store fixed-size collections of data, while strings offer robust character handling. The Collections Framework enhances Java's data manipulation capabilities, allowing you to choose the right data structure for your needs.

Understanding these concepts is fundamental for effective programming in Java, as they enable you to store, retrieve, and manage data efficiently, making your applications more powerful and flexible. As you continue to practice and explore these data structures, you'll be better equipped to handle a variety of programming challenges.

Chapter 5: Object-Oriented Programming Concepts

Object-Oriented Programming (OOP) is a programming paradigm that uses "objects" to represent data and methods to manipulate that data. Java, as a fully object-oriented programming language, leverages the principles of OOP to promote code reusability, modularity, and a more intuitive approach to software design. In this chapter, we will explore the core concepts of OOP in Java, including classes and objects, inheritance and polymorphism, encapsulation and abstraction, and interfaces and abstract classes.

Classes and Objects

What are Classes?

A class is a blueprint for creating objects. It defines a data structure that includes attributes (fields) and behaviors (methods). In Java, a class serves as a template that encapsulates data for the object.

Syntax for Defining a Class

Here's how you define a class in Java:

```java
public class Car {
    // Attributes (fields)
    String color;
    String model;
    int year;

    // Constructor
    public Car(String color, String model, int year) {
        this.color = color;
        this.model = model;
        this.year = year;
    }

    // Method
    public void displayInfo() {
        System.out.println("Car Model: " + model + ", Color: " + color + ", Year: " + year);
    }
}
```

Explanation:

The provided code defines a Java class named `Car`, which serves as a blueprint for creating car objects.

These are instance variables, also known as attributes or fields. They store the state of the `Car` object:

- `color`: A `String` representing the color of the car.
- `model`: A `String` representing the model of the car.

- `year`: An `int` representing the manufacturing year of the car.

public Car(String color, String model, int year) {

The constructor is a special method that is called when an object of the class is created. This constructor takes three parameters: `color`, `model`, and `year`.

Inside the constructor, the `this` keyword refers to the current object. It distinguishes between the instance variables and the parameters with the same name. The constructor initializes the attributes with the provided values.

public void displayInfo() :

This is a public method named `displayInfo`, which does not return any value (`void`).

When called, this method prints out the car's model, color, and year using the `System.out.println` function. It formats the output as a string, providing a clear summary of the car's attributes.

In summary, the `Car` class encapsulates the properties of a car (color, model, year) and provides a way to instantiate car objects with specific attributes through the constructor. The `displayInfo` method allows you to display the details of the car in a user-friendly format. This structure illustrates the principles of object-oriented programming, such as encapsulation and the use of constructors to initialize objects.

What are Objects?

An object is an instance of a class. When you create an object, you allocate memory for the attributes defined in the class and can invoke the methods associated with that class.

Creating Objects

To create an object, you use the `new` keyword followed by the class constructor:

```
public class Main {
    public static void main(String[] args) {

// Creating an object of the Car class
Car myCar = new Car("Red", "Toyota", 2021);
myCar.displayInfo();
    }
}
```

Output:

Car Model: Toyota, Color: Red, Year: 2021

Importance of Classes and Objects

Classes and objects allow you to model real-world entities. For instance, in the example above, the `Car` class represents a real-world car, while the `myCar` object represents a specific instance of that car. This encapsulation of data and behavior simplifies program management and enhances code reusability

Inheritance and Polymorphism

Inheritance

Inheritance is a mechanism that allows one class to inherit the attributes and methods of another class. This promotes code reuse and establishes a natural hierarchy between classes.

Types of Inheritance

1. **Single Inheritance**: A subclass inherits from one superclass.
2. **Multilevel Inheritance**: A subclass is derived from another subclass.
3. **Hierarchical Inheritance**: Multiple subclasses inherit from a single superclass.

Example of Inheritance

```java
// Superclass
public class Vehicle {
    String type;
    public Vehicle(String type) {
        this.type = type;
    }
    public void displayType() {
        System.out.println("Vehicle Type: " + type);
    }
}
// Subclass
public class Car extends Vehicle {
    String model;
    public Car(String type, String model) {
        super(type);
// Calling superclass constructor
```

```
        this.model = model;
    }

    public void displayInfo() {
        displayType();
        System.out.println("Car Model: " + model);
    }
}
```

Explanation:

The **Vehicle** class is a superclass with a **type** attribute and a method to display it.

The **Car** class extends **Vehicle**, adds a **model** attribute, and uses the superclass constructor, also providing a method to display both type and model.

Using Inheritance

You can create an object of the subclass and use both the inherited and subclass methods:

```
public class Main {

    public static void main(String[] args) {

        Car myCar = new Car("Sedan", "Toyota");

        myCar.displayInfo();

    }

}
```

Polymorphism

Polymorphism allows methods to do different things based on the object that it is acting upon. In Java, polymorphism is primarily achieved through method overriding and method overloading.

Method Overriding

When a subclass provides a specific implementation of a method that is already defined in its superclass, it is called method overriding.

```java
public class Animal {
    public void sound() {
        System.out.println("Animal makes a sound");
    }
}

public class Dog extends Animal {
    @Override
    public void sound() {
        System.out.println("Dog barks");
    }
}
```

Explanation:

Polymorphism allows the `Dog` class to override the `sound` method of its superclass `Animal`. When `sound` is called on a `Dog` object, it outputs "Dog barks," demonstrating dynamic method resolution based on the object's actual type.

Using Polymorphism

You can call the overridden method on a superclass reference:

```
public class Main {

    public static void main(String[] args) {

        Animal myDog = new Dog();

        myDog.sound(); // Output: Dog barks

    }

}
```

Benefits of Inheritance and Polymorphism

1. **Code Reusability**: You can reuse existing code without having to rewrite it.
2. **Dynamic Method Resolution**: The correct method is called at runtime, enhancing flexibility.
3. **Hierarchical Classification**: It models real-world relationships, making the code more intuitive.

Encapsulation and Abstraction

Encapsulation

Encapsulation is the practice of bundling the data (attributes) and methods (functions) that operate on the data into a single unit, typically a class. It restricts direct access to some of the object's components, which is a means of preventing accidental interference and misuse.

Access Modifiers

Java uses access modifiers to set the accessibility of classes, methods, and variables. The main modifiers are:

1. **public**: Accessible from anywhere.
2. **private**: Accessible only within the class.
3. **protected**: Accessible within the same package and subclasses.

Example of Encapsulation

```
public class BankAccount {

private double balance;

// Private variable

public BankAccount(double initialBalance)
{
```

```
        this.balance = initialBalance;

    }

    public void deposit(double amount) {

        if (amount > 0) {

            balance += amount;

        }

    }

    public double getBalance() {

        return balance;

    }

}
```

Explanation:

Encapsulation in the `BankAccount` class restricts direct access to the `balance` variable by declaring it as private. It provides public methods for depositing money and retrieving the balance, ensuring controlled access and protecting the account's integrity.

Abstraction

Abstraction is the concept of hiding the complex implementation details and exposing only the necessary features of an object. It helps in reducing programming complexity and increasing efficiency.

Abstract Classes and Methods

An abstract class cannot be instantiated and may contain abstract methods (methods without a body) that must be implemented by subclasses.

```
public abstract class Shape {
    abstract void draw();
// Abstract method
}

public class Circle extends Shape {
    void draw() {
          System.out.println("Drawing a Circle");
    }
}
```

Explanation:

Abstraction in the Shape class hides implementation details. The Circle subclass provides a specific draw method, allowing varied shapes to be represented while focusing on their essential characteristics.

Using Encapsulation and Abstraction

Encapsulation protects the integrity of the data by providing a controlled interface, while abstraction allows the programmer to focus on interactions at a higher level without needing to know the internal workings.

```
public class Main {
    public static void main(String[] args) {
        BankAccount account = new BankAccount(1000);
        account.deposit(500);
        System.out.println("Current Balance: " + account.getBalance());

        Shape shape = new Circle();
        shape.draw(); // Output: Drawing a Circle
    }
}
```

Explanation:

The `BankAccount` class uses encapsulation for balance control, while the `Shape` class demonstrates abstraction by allowing different shapes to be drawn without exposing implementation details.

Interfaces and Abstract Classes

Interfaces

An interface in Java is a reference type that can contain only constants, method signatures, default methods, static methods, and nested types. It cannot contain instance fields. Interfaces are used to achieve abstraction and multiple inheritance.

Defining an Interface

```
public interface Vehicle {
    void start(); // Method signature
    void stop();
}
```

Implementing an Interface

A class implements an interface by providing concrete implementations of its methods:

public class Car implements Vehicle {

  public void start() {

    System.out.println("Car started");

  }

```
    public void stop() {

        System.out.println("Car stopped");

    }

}
```

Explanation:

The `Vehicle` interface defines method signatures for `start` and `stop`. The `Car` class implements this interface by providing specific behaviors for these methods, allowing different vehicle types to share a common contract while defining their unique functionalities.

Using Interfaces

You can use the interface to refer to any object that implements it:

```
public class Main {

    public static void main(String[] args) {

        Vehicle myCar = new Car();

        myCar.start(); // Output: Car started
```

myCar.stop(); // Output: Car stopped

}

}

Abstract Classes vs. Interfaces

1. **Abstract Class**:
   - Can have both abstract and concrete methods.
   - Can have state (instance variables).
   - Supports single inheritance.
2. **Interface**:
   - Cannot have concrete methods (before Java 8; from Java 8, it can have default and static methods).
   - Cannot have state (only constants).
   - Supports multiple inheritance.

Conclusion

In this chapter, we delved into the core concepts of Object-Oriented Programming in Java. Understanding classes and objects is fundamental to structuring code effectively, while inheritance and polymorphism allow for code reusability and flexibility. Encapsulation and abstraction promote a cleaner interface and protect data integrity, and interfaces and abstract classes provide a way to achieve multiple inheritance and abstraction.

Mastering these OOP principles will enhance your ability to design and implement robust, maintainable Java applications. As you practice, you'll find that these concepts not only simplify your code but also make it more intuitive and easier to work with, ultimately leading to better software design and development.

Chapter 6: Exception Handling

Exception handling is a critical aspect of programming in Java, allowing developers to manage errors and exceptional conditions gracefully. This chapter explores the fundamental concepts of exceptions, how to use try-catch blocks for handling them, and how to create custom exceptions tailored to specific application needs.

Understanding Exceptions

An exception is an event that disrupts the normal flow of a program's execution. It can occur due to various reasons, such as invalid user input, unavailable resources, or arithmetic errors like division by zero. In Java, exceptions are represented as objects and are part of the Java Exception Hierarchy.

Java categorizes exceptions into two main types:

1. **Checked Exceptions**: These are exceptions that are checked at compile time. The compiler requires that they be either handled using a try-catch block or declared in the method signature with a `throws` clause. Examples include `IOException` and `SQLException`.

2. **Unchecked Exceptions**: These are exceptions that occur at runtime and are not checked at compile time. They are subclasses of `RuntimeException`. Common examples include `NullPointerException`, `ArrayIndexOutOfBoundsException`, and `ArithmeticException`. While these exceptions can be handled, it is often recommended to address the root cause to prevent them from occurring.

Understanding these types of exceptions helps developers to write robust code that can handle potential errors effectively.

Try-Catch Blocks

The primary mechanism for handling exceptions in Java is the try-catch block. This structure allows developers to write code that may throw exceptions while providing a way to catch and handle those exceptions when they occur.

Syntax

Here's the basic syntax of a try-catch block:

```
try {
    // Code that may throw an exception
} catch (ExceptionType e) {
    // Code to handle the exception
}
```

Example

Consider a scenario where we attempt to read a file that may not exist:

```java
import java.io.FileReader;
import java.io.IOException;

public class FileExample {
    public static void main(String[] args) {
        try {
            FileReader file = new FileReader("nonexistentfile.txt");
        } catch (IOException e) {
            System.out.println("File not found: " + e.getMessage());
        }
    }
}
```

In this example:

- The `try` block contains the code that attempts to open a file.
- If the file does not exist, an `IOException` is thrown.
- The `catch` block captures the exception and prints an appropriate message to the user.

Finally Block

Additionally, a `finally` block can be used after the catch block. This block is executed regardless of whether an exception occurred or not, making it ideal for cleanup activities, such as closing files or releasing resources.

```
try {
    // Code that may throw an exception
} catch (ExceptionType e) {
    // Handle exception
} finally {
    // Cleanup code
}
```

Creating Custom Exceptions

In some cases, the standard exceptions provided by Java may not be sufficient to convey specific error conditions relevant to an application. In such cases, developers can create custom exceptions.

How to Create a Custom Exception

To create a custom exception, follow these steps:

1. **Extend an Exception Class**: Custom exceptions should extend `Exception` for checked exceptions or `RuntimeException` for unchecked exceptions.
2. **Define Constructors**: Implement constructors that allow the passing of messages and/or causes.

Example

Here's how you can create a custom exception for an invalid account operation:

public class InvalidAccountOperationException extends Exception {

   public InvalidAccountOperationException(String message) {

     super(message);

   }

}

You can then use this custom exception in your application:

```
public class BankAccount {
    private double balance;

    public BankAccount(double balance) {
        this.balance = balance;
    }

    public void withdraw(double amount) throws InvalidAccountOperationException {
        if (amount > balance) {
            throw new InvalidAccountOperationException("Insufficient balance for withdrawal.");
        }
```

```
        balance -= amount;
    }
}
```

Handling Custom Exceptions

Using custom exceptions enhances the readability and maintainability of your code. You can catch and handle your custom exceptions just like standard exceptions, providing more specific error handling logic.

```
public class Main {
    public static void main(String[] args) {
        BankAccount account = new BankAccount(1000);
        try {
            account.withdraw(1500);
        } catch (InvalidAccountOperationException e) {
            System.out.println(e.getMessage());
        }
    }
}
```

Conclusion

Exception handling in Java is a powerful mechanism that allows developers to manage errors gracefully. By understanding the types of exceptions, effectively using try-catch blocks, and creating custom exceptions, developers can write robust applications that can handle unexpected situations without crashing. This not only improves the user experience but also aids in maintaining the integrity of the application. As you implement exception handling in your projects, remember to anticipate potential errors and plan accordingly to enhance the resilience of your code.

Chapter 7: Basic Input and Output

Basic input and output (I/O) in Java are crucial for user interaction and data management. This chapter explores console I/O, file I/O basics, and the use of Java's extensive I/O libraries.

Reading from and Writing to the Console

In Java, the `Scanner` class is commonly used for reading input from the console. It allows users to enter data that can be processed by the program. To use `Scanner`, you must import it from the `java.util` package. Here's a simple example:

```java
import java.util.Scanner;

public class ConsoleInput {
    public static void main(String[] args) {
        Scanner scanner = new Scanner(System.in);
        System.out.print("Enter your name: ");
        String name = scanner.nextLine();
        System.out.println("Hello, " + name + "!");
        scanner.close();
    }
}
```

File I/O Basics

Java provides robust file I/O capabilities through classes in the `java.io` package. You can read from and write to files using `FileReader` and `FileWriter`, along with buffering for efficient operations. For instance, to read from a file line by line, you can use `BufferedReader`:

```java
import java.io.BufferedReader;
import java.io.FileReader;
import java.io.IOException;

public class FileInput {
    public static void main(String[] args) {
        try (BufferedReader reader = new BufferedReader(new FileReader("file.txt"))) {
            String line;
            while ((line = reader.readLine()) != null) {
                System.out.println(line);
            }
        } catch (IOException e) {
            System.out.println("An error occurred: " + e.getMessage());
        }
    }
}
```

This example demonstrates reading a file named `file.txt`, printing each line to the console.

Using Java's I/O Libraries

Java's I/O libraries, particularly `java.nio.file` and `java.io`, provide a wide array of classes and methods for handling files, directories, and streams. The `java.nio.file` package includes classes for more modern file operations, such as `Path` and `Files`, which simplify file manipulation and improve performance with non-blocking I/O.

For example, using `Files` to read all lines from a file is straightforward:

```java
import java.nio.file.Files;
import java.nio.file.Paths;
import java.io.IOException;

public class NIOExample {
    public static void main(String[] args) {
        try {
            Files.lines(Paths.get("file.txt")).forEach(System.out::println);
        } catch (IOException e) {
            System.out.println("An error occurred: " + e.getMessage());
        }
    }
}
```

Chapter 8: Java Development Best Practices

Developing robust Java applications involves not just writing code but adhering to best practices that enhance readability, maintainability, and overall software quality. This chapter covers key areas such as code conventions and formatting, debugging techniques, and strategies for writing clean and maintainable code.

Code Conventions and Formatting

Adhering to code conventions is crucial in any development project. Java has established conventions that promote uniformity and readability. Key conventions include:

1. **Naming Conventions**:
    - **Classes** should use CamelCase (e.g., `CustomerAccount`).
    - **Methods** and **variables** should use camelCase (e.g., `calculateTotal`).
    - **Constants** should be in uppercase with underscores (e.g., `MAX_COUNT`).
2. **Indentation and Spacing**:

- Use four spaces for indentation to improve readability.
- Maintain consistent spacing around operators and between code blocks to make code easier to scan.

3. **Braces**:
   - Opening braces should be placed at the end of the line for class and method declarations and on a new line for control structures (if, for, while).
   - This enhances visibility and distinguishes between block levels.

4. **Comments**:
   - Use comments judiciously to explain complex logic. Javadoc comments (/** ... */) should be used for public classes and methods to generate documentation.

By following these conventions, teams can ensure that their codebases are accessible and understandable, regardless of who authored the code.

Debugging Techniques

Effective debugging is essential for identifying and resolving issues in Java applications. Here are some practical debugging techniques:

1. **Use of Logging**:

- Implement logging instead of relying solely on print statements. Java's `java.util.logging` package or third-party libraries like Log4j and SLF4J can help you log messages with varying levels of severity (info, debug, error).
- This allows you to track application behavior in production without cluttering the console.

2. **Integrated Development Environment (IDE) Tools**:
    - Leverage IDE features such as breakpoints, watches, and step-through debugging to inspect the state of your application while it runs.
    - Tools like Eclipse, IntelliJ IDEA, and NetBeans provide powerful debugging capabilities, allowing you to analyze variables and flow control effectively.

3. **Unit Testing**:
    - Writing unit tests helps catch errors early in the development process. Frameworks like JUnit and TestNG enable you to create tests that validate individual components.
    - Running these tests frequently can help identify regressions and ensure that new changes don't introduce bugs.

4. **Error Handling**:
    - Implement proper error handling using exceptions. Instead of allowing your application to crash, catch exceptions and handle them gracefully, providing

meaningful error messages to users and logging relevant information for developers.

Writing Clean and Maintainable Code

Writing clean code is a hallmark of professional software development. Here are key principles to consider:

1. **Single Responsibility Principle (SRP)**:
    - Each class and method should have a single responsibility. This promotes separation of concerns and makes the code easier to understand and test.
    - For example, a class that handles user authentication should not also manage user interface elements.
2. **DRY Principle (Don't Repeat Yourself)**:
    - Avoid duplicating code. If you find yourself writing the same code in multiple places, consider refactoring it into a single method or class.
    - This not only reduces errors but also makes future updates easier since changes need to be made in one location.
3. **Use Meaningful Names**:
    - Choose descriptive names for classes, methods, and variables. A method called `calculateTotal` clearly

indicates its purpose compared to a vague name like `doStuff`.
  - This practice significantly enhances code readability.
4. **Refactoring**:
   - Regularly refactor your code to improve structure and readability without changing its functionality. This includes breaking large methods into smaller ones, renaming variables for clarity, and removing unused code.
5. **Code Reviews**:
   - Conduct regular code reviews with your team. Peer reviews help identify issues, share knowledge, and enforce coding standards.
   - Collaborative feedback can lead to better coding practices and enhanced code quality.
6. **Consistent Structure**:
   - Maintain a consistent project structure. Group related classes into packages and organize files logically. This makes it easier to navigate and understand the project.

Conclusion

Following best practices in Java development is essential for creating high-quality software. By adhering to code conventions and formatting, employing effective debugging techniques, and striving to write clean and maintainable code, developers can enhance their productivity and ensure that their applications are robust and scalable. These practices not only improve individual projects but also foster a culture of excellence within development teams, ultimately leading to more successful software solutions.

Chapter 9: Next Steps in Java Development

As you advance in your Java development journey, exploring additional resources, advanced concepts, and practical projects is essential for growth.

Learning Resources and Communities

Numerous online resources are available for further learning. Websites like Codecademy, Coursera, and Udemy offer structured courses that cover various aspects of Java, from basic to advanced levels. Official documentation at Oracle's Java site is invaluable for understanding language features and libraries.

Joining online communities, such as Stack Overflow, Reddit's r/java, or Java-focused Discord servers, allows you to engage with other developers. These platforms provide opportunities to ask questions, share knowledge, and stay updated on industry trends.

Advanced Java Concepts to Explore

After mastering the basics, consider delving into advanced concepts like:

1. **Multithreading and Concurrency**: Learn how to write efficient applications that perform multiple tasks simultaneously, improving performance and responsiveness.
2. **Java Streams and Functional Programming**: Explore the Stream API for handling data in a more functional style, which can lead to cleaner and more concise code.
3. **Java EE and Spring Framework**: Investigate enterprise-level applications using Java EE or the Spring framework for building robust, scalable web applications.
4. **Design Patterns**: Familiarize yourself with common design patterns that can help you solve recurring design problems effectively.

Building Your Portfolio and Projects

Creating a portfolio is vital for showcasing your skills to potential employers. Work on diverse projects that highlight your abilities, such as:

- Web applications using Spring Boot.
- Mobile apps with Java for Android.
- Open-source contributions on platforms like GitHub.

Document your projects, include code samples, and describe your problem-solving process. This not only demonstrates your technical skills but also your ability to communicate effectively. Building a strong portfolio will significantly enhance your job prospects and opportunities in the tech industry.

Chapter 10: Conclusion

As we wrap up this exploration of Java development, it's important to reflect on the key concepts covered and look ahead to your ongoing learning journey.

Recap of Key Concepts

Throughout this guide, you have learned the fundamentals of Java programming, including object-oriented programming principles, basic syntax, and data structures like arrays, lists, and maps. We discussed essential concepts such as exception handling, file I/O, and the importance of writing clean, maintainable code. You also gained insights into Java development best practices, including debugging techniques and adhering to coding conventions.

Staying Motivated and Continuing Your Learning Journey

The journey in software development is continuous, and staying motivated is key. Set clear, achievable goals for your learning. Whether you aim to master specific frameworks like Spring or delve into advanced topics like multithreading, having a roadmap helps you maintain focus.

Engage with the community by participating in forums, attending meetups, or joining coding groups. Collaboration and networking with fellow developers can provide inspiration and support, making the learning process more enjoyable.

Regularly challenge yourself with new projects that push your boundaries. Consider contributing to open-source projects or developing personal applications that interest you. This practical experience not only solidifies your skills but also enhances your portfolio.

Lastly, embrace the mindset of lifelong learning. Technology evolves rapidly, and staying updated with the latest developments in Java and programming practices is crucial. Utilize online courses, books, and tutorials to continually expand your knowledge base.

By integrating these strategies, you'll cultivate a fulfilling and rewarding journey in Java development, paving the way for a successful career in technology.

www.ingramcontent.com/pod-product-compliance
Lightning Source LLC
Chambersburg PA
CBHW070118230526
45472CB00004B/1309